*M*ay

you

find

solace

as you grieve the loss of

_____

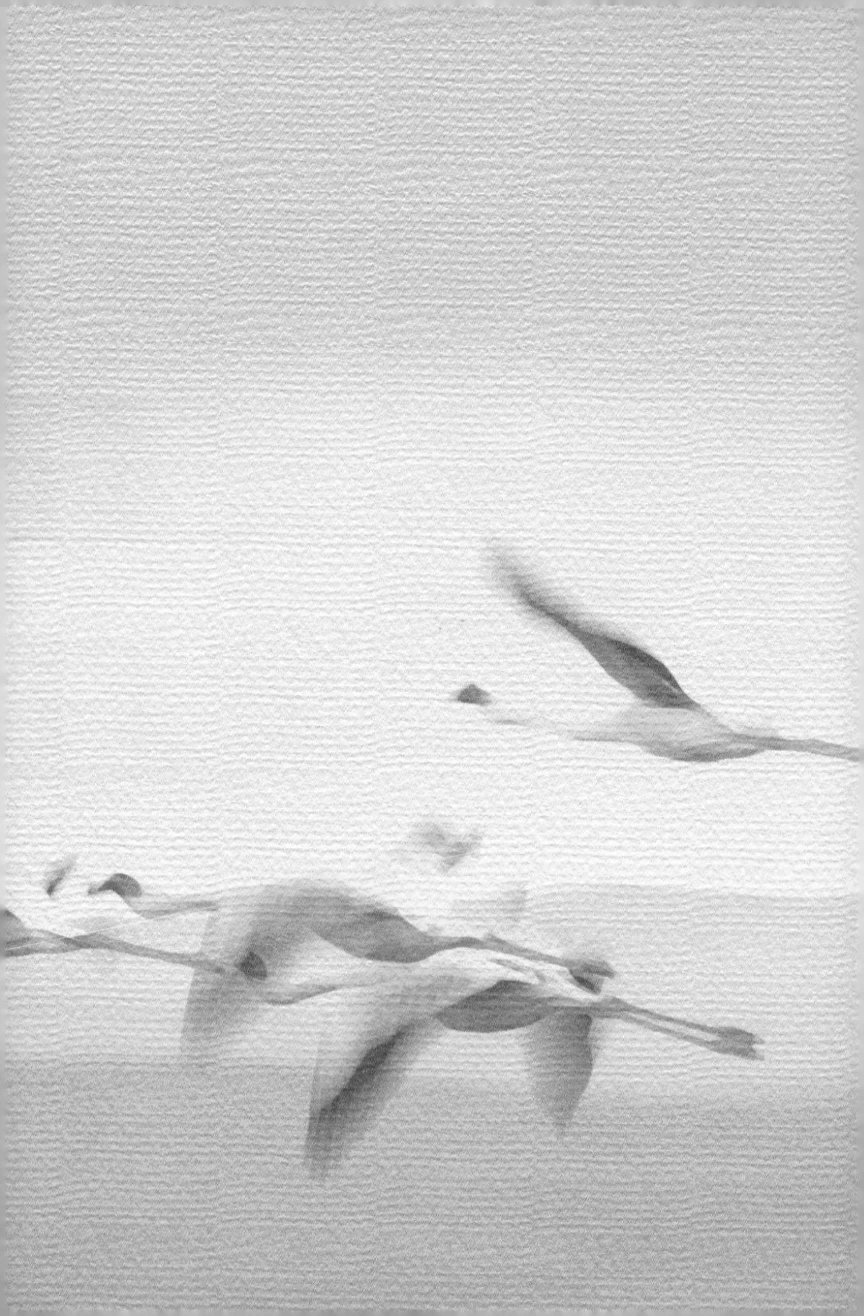

May your circle of understanding and caring persons be many, and may you allow them to support and sustain you in your sadness.

*M*ay you rest your

heartache in the compassionate

arms of God each day and find

comfort from this Enduring Love.

May you welcome the tears you shed as friends of your soul, gifting you with an opening to release your pain.

May disappointment, anger, guilt, or any other hurts that cling to you be acknowledged and set free.

May you trust the hidden part of you where your resilience resides and remember often the inner strength your spirit contains.

May you find the balance you need between activity and quiet so you can be attentive to your grief.

May you be gentle

and compassionate with

yourself by caring well for

your body, mind, and spirit.

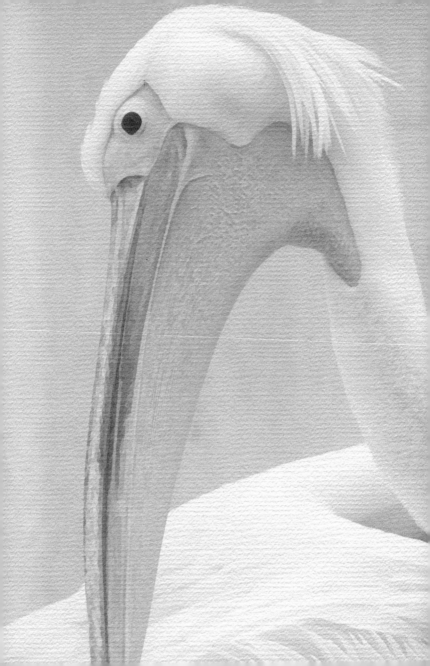

May you believe in your ability to eventually heal from your loss, no matter how much loneliness or desolation you now experience.

May you have the

necessary energy to focus on

the details of life that must be

done, in spite of how you feel.

May the day come when memories of your departed one bring you more comfort than sadness.

May the empty hollow in you grow less wide and deep as you receive touches of consolation and assurances of peace.

May you be healed
from your grief and extend
your compassion generously to
others who hurt.

May you recognize when it is time for you to let go and move on, doing so when your grief has faded and you are ready to allow the past to be at rest.

May you trust that love is stronger than death and draw comfort from the bond that unites you with your loved one.